# 42 Coffee and Tea Recipes for Home

By: Kelly Johnson

**Table of Contents**

Coffee Recipes

- Classic Black Coffee
- Espresso Shot
- Cappuccino
- Latte
- Americano
- Mocha
- Affogato
- Iced Coffee
- Cold Brew
- Nitro Cold Brew
- Turkish Coffee
- Viennese Coffee
- Irish Coffee
- Mexican Spiced Coffee
- Coconut Iced Coffee
- Hazelnut Macchiato
- Salted Caramel Latte
- Pumpkin Spice Latte
- Maple Pecan Coffee
- Almond Joy Coffee
- Gingerbread Latte

Tea Recipes

- Classic Earl Grey Lavender Tea

- Chai Latte with Spiced Honey
- Matcha Green Tea Smoothie
- Jasmine Rose White Tea
- Minty Moroccan Mint Tea
- Turmeric Ginger Herbal Tea
- Berry Hibiscus Iced Tea
- Berry hibiscus Iced Tea
- Lemon Chamomile Relaxation Tea
- Peach Basil White Tea Cooler
- Lavender Blueberry Green Tea
- Masala Rooibos Chai
- Coconut Almond Black Chai
- Vanilla Rooibos Latte
- Ginger Peach Turmeric Iced Tea
- Citrus Mint Green Tea Punch
- Cucumber Basil White Tea Refresher
- Rose Cardamom Black Tea Elixir
- Pineapple Ginger Herbal Infusion
- Maple Pecan Oolong Tea
- Blue Butterfly Pea Flower Tea
- Chocolate Mint Rooibos Bliss

# Coffee Recipes:

**Classic Black Coffee**

Ingredients:

- Freshly ground coffee beans (medium grind)
- Water
- Optional: Sugar, cream, or milk (to taste)

Instructions:

Measure the Coffee:
- Use about 1 to 2 tablespoons of coffee grounds for every 6 ounces of water. Adjust according to your taste preferences.

Grind the Coffee:
- Grind the coffee beans just before brewing to ensure freshness. For black coffee, a medium grind is generally suitable.

Water Measurement:
- Measure the water based on the number of cups of coffee you want. Remember, 1 cup is approximately 6 ounces.

Boil the Water:
- Boil the water using a kettle or another suitable method. Make sure the water is fresh and clean for the best flavor.

Prepare the Coffee Maker:
- If you're using a drip coffee maker, place the coffee grounds in the filter. If using a French press, put the coffee grounds directly into the press.

Pour Hot Water:
- Once the water reaches the desired temperature, pour it over the coffee grounds. Ensure that the coffee grounds are evenly saturated.

Brew the Coffee:
- Allow the coffee to brew. This may take a few minutes depending on the brewing method you're using. For drip coffee makers, follow the machine's instructions.

Serve:
- Once the brewing is complete, pour the black coffee into your favorite mug.

Optional Additions:
- Customize your black coffee by adding sugar, cream, or milk according to your taste preferences. However, if you want to enjoy the pure, unadulterated taste of black coffee, skip these additions.

Enjoy:

- Sip and savor your classic black coffee! Adjust the strength and flavor by experimenting with the coffee-to-water ratio until you find the perfect balance for your taste.

Feel free to adjust the measurements and steps based on your personal preferences and the type of coffee maker you have. Enjoy your classic black coffee!

**Espresso Shot**

Ingredients:

- Freshly ground espresso beans
- Water

Equipment:

- Espresso machine
- Burr grinder
- Tamper

Instructions:

Preheat the Espresso Machine:
- Turn on your espresso machine and allow it to fully heat up. This is crucial for extracting the flavors properly.

Grind the Espresso Beans:
- Use a burr grinder to grind the espresso beans just before brewing. The grind should be fine and uniform, similar to powdered sugar.

Dose the Coffee:
- Measure out the appropriate amount of coffee grounds for a single or double shot, depending on your preference and machine capabilities. A standard single shot is around 7-9 grams, while a double shot is around 14-18 grams.

Tamp the Coffee:

- Place the coffee grounds into the portafilter and use a tamper to compact the grounds evenly. Apply firm and even pressure to ensure a smooth and consistent extraction.

Insert the Portafilter:

- Insert the portafilter into the machine's group head and start the extraction process immediately.

Brew the Espresso Shot:

- Activate the espresso machine to start the brewing process. The water should be forced through the compacted coffee grounds under high pressure. The extraction time for a standard espresso shot is typically around 25-30 seconds.

Watch the Flow:

- During extraction, observe the flow of the espresso. It should start with a slow drip and gradually turn into a steady, thick stream. A well-pulled espresso shot will have a layer of crema on top, which is a golden-brown, frothy layer.

Serve Immediately:

- Once the extraction is complete, serve the espresso shot immediately in a pre-warmed espresso cup.

Enjoy:

- Sip and savor your rich and concentrated espresso shot. Feel free to enjoy it as is or use it as the base for other espresso-based drinks like lattes, cappuccinos, or Americanos.

Remember, the key to a good espresso shot is using freshly ground coffee, proper tamping, and maintaining the right brewing parameters. Adjust the grind size, dose, and extraction time based on your preferences and the characteristics of your espresso machine.

**Cappuccino**

Ingredients:

- Freshly ground espresso beans
- Water
- Milk

Equipment:

- Espresso machine
- Burr grinder
- Milk frother or steamer
- Tamper

Instructions:

Prepare the Espresso Shot:
- Follow the steps outlined in the espresso shot recipe to prepare a strong and flavorful shot of espresso.

Froth the Milk:
- Pour the desired amount of milk into the frothing pitcher. The amount of milk depends on your preference, but a standard cappuccino usually consists of equal parts espresso, steamed milk, and frothed milk.
- Use the milk frother or steamer to froth the milk. Hold the steam wand just below the surface of the milk and turn on the steam. Froth the milk until it reaches a creamy and velvety texture with a good amount of foam.

Tap and Swirl:

- Tap the bottom of the frothing pitcher on a countertop to eliminate any large bubbles. Swirl the pitcher to integrate the frothed and steamed milk.

Pour the Milk:

- Pour the steamed milk over the prepared espresso shot. Aim for an even distribution of milk in the cup.

Add Frothed Milk:

- Spoon the frothed milk on top of the cappuccino to create a layer of thick foam.

Dusting (Optional):

- If desired, you can sprinkle a small amount of cocoa powder, cinnamon, or nutmeg on top of the foam for added flavor and presentation.

Serve Immediately:

- Cappuccinos are best enjoyed right away while the espresso is fresh, and the milk is creamy and frothy.

Enjoy:

- Sip and enjoy your homemade cappuccino! Adjust the milk-to-espresso ratio and foam level to suit your taste preferences.

Feel free to experiment with the milk type (whole milk, skim milk, soy milk, etc.) and the level of foam to create a cappuccino that suits your taste.

**Latte**

Ingredients:

- Freshly ground espresso beans
- Water
- Milk

Equipment:

- Espresso machine
- Burr grinder
- Milk frother or steamer
- Tamper

Instructions:

Prepare the Espresso Shot:
- Follow the steps outlined in the espresso shot recipe to prepare a strong and flavorful shot of espresso.

Froth the Milk:
- Pour the desired amount of milk into the frothing pitcher. The amount of milk depends on your preference, but a latte typically has more steamed milk and less foam compared to a cappuccino.
- Use the milk frother or steamer to froth and steam the milk. Hold the steam wand just below the surface of the milk and turn on the steam. Froth the milk until it reaches a creamy texture, with a small amount of foam.

Tap and Swirl:
- Tap the bottom of the frothing pitcher on a countertop to eliminate any large bubbles. Swirl the pitcher to mix the frothed and steamed milk.

Pour the Milk:
- Pour the steamed milk over the prepared espresso shot. Hold back the foam with a spoon to control the amount of foam in your latte.

Add a Touch of Foam:
- Spoon a small amount of foam on top of the latte for a little extra creaminess.

Serve Immediately:
- Lattes are best enjoyed promptly while the espresso is fresh and the milk is smooth and velvety.

Optional Flavors (Optional):
- If desired, you can add flavored syrups such as vanilla, caramel, or hazelnut to your latte for additional sweetness and flavor.

Enjoy:
- Sip and enjoy your homemade latte! Adjust the milk-to-espresso ratio and foam level to suit your taste preferences.

Feel free to customize your latte by experimenting with different milk types, adjusting the level of foam, and adding your favorite flavored syrups.

**Americano**

Ingredients:

- Freshly ground espresso beans
- Water

Equipment:

- Espresso machine
- Burr grinder
- Hot water dispenser or kettle

Instructions:

Prepare the Espresso Shot(s):
- Follow the steps outlined in the espresso shot recipe to prepare one or two shots of espresso, depending on your preference.

Boil Water:
- While the espresso is brewing, boil water using a kettle or another suitable method. The amount of water will depend on how strong you want your Americano. A common ratio is 1:1, meaning equal parts espresso and hot water.

Combine Espresso and Hot Water:
- In a cup or mug, pour the freshly brewed espresso shot(s).
- Add hot water to the espresso. Start by adding the hot water slowly and taste as you go to find the strength that suits your preference. If you're

using a 1:1 ratio, you would add an equal amount of hot water to the espresso.

Adjust Strength:

- Customize the strength of your Americano by adding more or less hot water until you achieve your desired flavor.

Optional Additions (Optional):

- If you like, you can add sugar, cream, or milk to your Americano, though traditionally it's served black.

Stir (Optional):

- Give the Americano a gentle stir to ensure that the espresso and hot water are well combined.

Serve Immediately:

- Americanos are best enjoyed promptly while the espresso is fresh and the beverage is hot.

Enjoy:

- Sip and savor your classic Americano! The result should be a smooth, diluted coffee with a flavor profile similar to drip coffee.

Feel free to experiment with the espresso-to-water ratio to find the strength that you enjoy the most. Americanos are a versatile drink that you can easily adjust to match your taste preferences.

**Mocha**

Ingredients:

- Freshly ground espresso beans
- Water
- Milk
- Chocolate syrup or cocoa powder
- Whipped cream (optional)

Equipment:

- Espresso machine
- Burr grinder
- Milk frother or steamer
- Tamper

Instructions:

Prepare the Espresso Shot:
- Follow the steps outlined in the espresso shot recipe to prepare a strong and flavorful shot of espresso.

Froth the Milk:
- Pour the desired amount of milk into the frothing pitcher. The amount of milk depends on your preference, but for a mocha, you typically want a balance between the espresso and the milk.
- Use the milk frother or steamer to froth and steam the milk. Aim for a creamy texture with a moderate amount of foam.

Add Chocolate:

- Stir in chocolate syrup or cocoa powder into the freshly brewed espresso. The amount of chocolate can be adjusted based on your sweetness preference. Start with about 1 to 2 tablespoons of chocolate syrup or 1 to 2 teaspoons of cocoa powder.

Combine Espresso and Chocolate:

- Mix the chocolate and espresso well to ensure the chocolate is fully dissolved.

Pour the Milk:

- Pour the frothed milk over the chocolate-infused espresso. Hold back the foam with a spoon to control the amount of foam in your mocha.

Optional Whipped Cream (Optional):

- If you like, you can top your mocha with a dollop of whipped cream for an extra indulgent treat.

Drizzle with Chocolate (Optional):

- For added visual appeal, you can drizzle a little extra chocolate syrup on top of the whipped cream.

Serve Immediately:

- Mochas are best enjoyed promptly while the espresso is fresh, the milk is velvety, and any whipped cream is still fluffy.

Enjoy:

- Sip and enjoy your delicious homemade mocha! Adjust the chocolate and milk ratios to suit your taste preferences.

Feel free to get creative with your mocha by experimenting with different types of chocolate or adding flavored syrups for additional depth of flavor.

**Affogato**

Ingredients:

- Freshly brewed espresso (1-2 shots per serving)
- Vanilla ice cream or gelato (1 scoop per serving)

Instructions:

Brew Espresso:

- Start by brewing one or two shots of espresso per serving. The espresso should be hot and freshly brewed.

Prepare the Ice Cream:

- Place one scoop of vanilla ice cream or gelato in a serving glass or cup. You can use a traditional ice cream scoop or a small disher.

Pour Espresso:

- Immediately after brewing the espresso, pour it over the scoop of vanilla ice cream. The hot espresso will begin to melt the ice cream, creating a delicious combination of hot and cold.

Serve Immediately:

- Affogatos are best enjoyed right away while the espresso is hot and the ice cream is still slightly firm.

Optional Additions (Optional):

- If you like, you can customize your affogato by adding a drizzle of chocolate syrup, a sprinkle of cocoa powder, or a dash of flavored liqueur like amaretto or hazelnut.

Enjoy:

- Use a spoon to enjoy the affogato by combining the melted ice cream and the rich espresso in each bite. The contrast of the hot espresso and cold ice cream is what makes this dessert so delightful.

Affogatos are incredibly versatile, and you can experiment with different ice cream flavors to create unique variations. Feel free to get creative and enjoy this simple yet elegant Italian treat!

**Iced Coffee**

Ingredients:

- Freshly ground coffee beans
- Water
- Ice cubes
- Optional: Sweetener, milk, cream, flavored syrups (to taste)

Equipment:

- Coffee maker (drip, pour-over, or cold brew)
- Burr grinder (if grinding your own coffee)
- Ice cubes
- Glass or pitcher

Instructions:

Brew Coffee:
- Brew a pot of strong coffee using your preferred method. You can use a drip coffee maker, pour-over method, or cold brew. If making hot coffee, you can brew it at double strength since it will be diluted by the ice.

Cool the Coffee:
- Allow the brewed coffee to cool to room temperature. You can speed up the cooling process by placing it in the refrigerator or pouring it over ice.

Prepare Ice Cubes:

- If you want to prevent your iced coffee from becoming too diluted, consider making coffee ice cubes by freezing some of your brewed coffee in an ice cube tray.

Fill Glass with Ice:

- Fill a glass with plenty of ice cubes. If you have coffee ice cubes, it's a great way to keep your iced coffee cold without diluting it.

Pour Coffee Over Ice:

- Pour the cooled or chilled coffee over the ice in the glass.

Add Optional Ingredients (Optional):

- Customize your iced coffee by adding sweeteners like sugar or simple syrup, and adjust the level of creaminess by adding milk or cream. You can also add flavored syrups for additional taste.

Stir:

- Use a long spoon to stir the iced coffee, ensuring that any added ingredients are well mixed.

Serve Immediately:

- Iced coffee is best enjoyed immediately while it's cold and refreshing.

Enjoy:

- Sip and enjoy your homemade iced coffee! Customize it to your liking by experimenting with different coffee-to-ice ratios and flavor additions.

Feel free to get creative with your iced coffee by trying different coffee varieties and experimenting with various flavorings and toppings. Whether you prefer it sweetened, creamy, or black, iced coffee is a versatile and delightful drink.

**Cold Brew**

Ingredients:

- Coarsely ground coffee beans
- Cold or room temperature water
- Ice cubes (optional)
- Milk, cream, or sweeteners (optional, for serving)

Equipment:

- Coarse coffee grinder
- Large jar or pitcher
- Fine mesh sieve or cheesecloth
- Additional container for straining

Instructions:

Grind Coffee Beans:
- Grind coarsely. The grind size is crucial for cold brew, as a finer grind may result in over-extraction and a bitter taste. Aim for a consistency similar to breadcrumbs.

Combine Coffee and Water:
- In a large jar or pitcher, combine the coarsely ground coffee with cold or room temperature water. Use a ratio of about 1 cup of coffee grounds to 4 cups of water as a starting point. Adjust according to your taste preferences.

Stir and Steep:

- Stir the coffee and water mixture to ensure all the grounds are saturated. Cover the container and let it steep in the refrigerator for at least 12 to 24 hours. The longer the steeping time, the stronger and more concentrated the cold brew will be.

Strain the Coffee:

- After the steeping period, strain the cold brew to separate the coffee grounds. You can use a fine mesh sieve or cheesecloth placed over another container or pitcher.

Optional Second Strain (Optional):

- For a smoother texture, you can perform a second strain using a paper coffee filter or a specialized cold brew filter.

Serve:

- Dilute the concentrated cold brew with water or milk according to your preference. You can serve it over ice cubes if desired.

Optional Additions (Optional):

- Customize your cold brew by adding milk, cream, sweeteners, or flavored syrups.

Enjoy:

- Sip and enjoy the smooth, full-bodied flavor of your homemade cold brew coffee!

Remember, cold brew is concentrated, so you may need to dilute it with water or milk before serving, depending on your taste preference. Experiment with the coffee-to-water ratio and steeping time to find the strength you enjoy the most. Cold brew is known for its milder acidity and smooth taste, making it a favorite among coffee enthusiasts.

**Turkish Coffee**

Ingredients:

- Finely ground Turkish coffee (approximately 1-2 heaping teaspoons per serving)
- Cold water
- Sugar (optional)
- Cardamom (optional)

Equipment:

- Turkish coffee pot (cezve)
- Small demitasse cups

Instructions:

Measure Ingredients:
- Measure the cold water using the coffee cup you plan to use. Typically, one cup of water is used for each serving.

Grind Coffee:
- Grind the coffee beans to a very fine, powder-like consistency. The grind is crucial for Turkish coffee, as the fine particles remain in the coffee and contribute to its unique flavor.

Add Water and Coffee to the Cezve:
- Add the measured cold water to the Turkish coffee pot (cezve). For each cup, add 1-2 heaping teaspoons of finely ground coffee to the water. Adjust the amount of coffee according to your taste preferences, considering that Turkish coffee is strong and intense.

Add Sugar and Cardamom (Optional):

- If you prefer sweetened or flavored coffee, you can add sugar to taste before placing the cezve on the heat. Additionally, a pinch of ground cardamom can be added for extra flavor.

Stir and Dissolve:

- Stir the coffee and sugar (if using) thoroughly in the cold water until the coffee is mostly dissolved.

Heat Slowly:

- Place the cezve over low heat. The key to Turkish coffee is to heat it slowly to allow the flavors to meld. Avoid stirring once the cezve is on the heat.

Foam Formation:

- As the coffee heats, it will begin to froth and form a layer of foam. This is a desirable characteristic of Turkish coffee.

Do Not Boil:

- Be careful not to let the coffee boil over. When it starts to foam and rise, reduce the heat to maintain a gentle simmer.

Pour Carefully:

- Once the coffee is ready, pour it carefully into the demitasse cups, making sure to distribute the foam evenly.

Wait and Enjoy:

- Allow the coffee grounds to settle at the bottom of the cup before sipping. Turkish coffee is traditionally served with a glass of cold water to cleanse the palate between sips.

Enjoy the rich and intense flavor of your homemade Turkish coffee. It's a unique and cultural way to experience the pleasures of coffee.

**Viennese Coffee**

Ingredients:

- Freshly ground coffee beans
- Water
- Whipped cream
- Sugar (optional)
- Chocolate shavings or cocoa powder (for garnish, optional)

Equipment:

- Coffee maker (drip or espresso machine)
- Whipped cream dispenser or hand mixer
- Demitasse cups

Instructions:

Brew Coffee:
- Brew a strong cup of coffee using your preferred method. Viennese coffee is often made with espresso, but you can also use strong drip coffee.

Sweeten Coffee (Optional):
- Add sugar to the hot coffee to sweeten it, adjusting the amount to your taste preferences. Stir until the sugar is fully dissolved.

Prepare Whipped Cream:
- While the coffee is brewing, prepare the whipped cream. You can use a whipped cream dispenser or a hand mixer. If using a dispenser, follow the instructions for loading the cream and charging it with nitrous oxide.

Whip the Cream:

- Whip the cream until it forms stiff peaks. You want the whipped cream to be thick and luxurious.

Serve Coffee:

- Pour the brewed and sweetened coffee into demitasse cups.

Top with Whipped Cream:

- Add a generous dollop of whipped cream on top of the coffee. The whipped cream should float on the surface of the coffee.

Garnish (Optional):

- If desired, sprinkle chocolate shavings or a dusting of cocoa powder over the whipped cream for an extra touch of flavor and decoration.

Serve Immediately:

- Viennese coffee is best enjoyed promptly while the coffee is hot and the whipped cream is still fluffy.

Enjoy:

- Sip and savor your Viennese coffee, enjoying the rich combination of strong coffee and velvety whipped cream.

Viennese coffee is a luxurious treat often associated with coffeehouses in Vienna, and it's a delightful way to indulge in a rich and creamy coffee experience. Adjust the sweetness, whipped cream quantity, and optional garnishes to suit your taste preferences.

**Irish Coffee**

Ingredients:

- Hot brewed coffee (strong)
- 1 to 1.5 ounces (30 to 45 ml) Irish whiskey
- 1 to 2 teaspoons brown sugar (adjust to taste)
- Whipped cream

Equipment:

- Irish coffee mug or heatproof glass
- Coffee maker
- Whisk or spoon for stirring
- Whipped cream dispenser or hand mixer

Instructions:

Brew Coffee:
- Brew a strong cup of hot coffee using your preferred method. Irish Coffee is traditionally made with strong black coffee.

Preheat the Glass:
- Preheat your Irish coffee mug or heatproof glass by rinsing it with hot water. Discard the hot water.

Add Sugar and Whiskey:
- Add 1 to 2 teaspoons of brown sugar to the preheated glass. Adjust the amount based on your sweetness preference.
- Pour 1 to 1.5 ounces (30 to 45 ml) of Irish whiskey into the glass.

Stir:
- Stir the mixture well to dissolve the sugar in the hot coffee.

Add Coffee:
- Pour the hot brewed coffee into the glass, leaving some space at the top.

Prepare Whipped Cream:
- While the coffee is brewing, prepare the whipped cream. You can use a whipped cream dispenser or a hand mixer. If using a dispenser, follow the instructions for loading the cream and charging it with nitrous oxide.

Whip the Cream:
- Whip the cream until it forms stiff peaks. The cream should be thick enough to float on top of the coffee.

Layer Whipped Cream:
- Gently float a layer of whipped cream on top of the hot coffee. You can pour it over the back of a spoon to help create a distinct layer.

Serve Immediately:
- Irish Coffee is best enjoyed promptly while the coffee is hot and the whipped cream is still fluffy.

Enjoy:
- Sip and enjoy the warmth and richness of your Irish Coffee with the delightful combination of coffee, whiskey, and cream.

Irish Coffee is a classic after-dinner drink or a comforting beverage for a chilly evening. Adjust the whiskey and sugar amounts to suit your taste, and savor this timeless cocktail.

**Mexican Spiced Coffee**

Ingredients:

- Freshly ground coffee beans
- Water
- Ground cinnamon
- Ground nutmeg
- Cocoa powder
- Brown sugar or sweetener of your choice
- Milk or cream (optional)

Equipment:

- Coffee maker
- Ground coffee filter
- Optional: Frother or steamer for milk

Instructions:

Brew Coffee:
- Brew a pot of coffee using your preferred method. Use a medium to dark roast for a bolder flavor.

Add Spices:
- While the coffee is brewing, mix in the following spices to your taste:
    - 1/4 to 1/2 teaspoon ground cinnamon
    - A pinch of ground nutmeg
    - 1 to 2 teaspoons cocoa powder

- Adjust the quantities based on your preference for spiciness and richness.

Sweeten Coffee:

- Add brown sugar or your preferred sweetener to the brewed coffee. Adjust the sweetness to your liking.

Stir Well:

- Stir the coffee thoroughly to ensure that the spices and sweetener are well incorporated.

Optional Milk or Cream:

- If desired, add milk or cream to your coffee for added richness. You can heat and froth the milk using a frother or steamer if you want a latte-like texture.

Garnish (Optional):

- Sprinkle a little extra cinnamon or cocoa powder on top for a decorative touch.

Serve Hot:

- Pour the spiced coffee into your favorite mug and enjoy it while it's hot.

Enjoy:

- Sip and savor the warm and aromatic flavors of Mexican Spiced Coffee!

Feel free to adjust the spice levels and sweetness according to your taste preferences. This Mexican-inspired coffee is a delightful way to enjoy the rich warmth of coffee with the added kick of spices.

**Coconut Iced Coffee**

Ingredients:

- Freshly ground coffee beans
- Water
- Coconut milk or coconut cream
- Sweetener of your choice (optional)
- Ice cubes
- Optional: Coconut flakes or shredded coconut for garnish

Equipment:

- Coffee maker
- Ground coffee filter
- Ice cube tray
- Blender (optional)

Instructions:

Brew Coffee:

- Brew a pot of strong coffee using your preferred method. A medium to dark roast works well for this recipe.

Cool the Coffee:

- Allow the brewed coffee to cool to room temperature. You can speed up the cooling process by placing it in the refrigerator.

Prepare Coconut Milk or Cream:

- Shake or stir the can of coconut milk or cream well to ensure it's properly mixed. You can also use a homemade coconut milk alternative.

Sweeten (Optional):

- If desired, add a sweetener of your choice to the cooled coffee. This can be sugar, honey, agave syrup, or a sugar substitute. Adjust the sweetness to your liking.

Combine Coffee and Coconut Milk:

- In a glass, mix the cooled coffee with coconut milk or cream. Use a ratio that suits your taste preferences. A common starting point is 1:1, but you can adjust it to be creamier or lighter.

Stir Well:

- Stir the coffee and coconut milk mixture thoroughly to ensure they are well combined.

Add Ice Cubes:

- Fill the glass with ice cubes. You can use regular ice cubes or make coffee ice cubes for an extra burst of coffee flavor.

Garnish (Optional):

- If you like, garnish the Coconut Iced Coffee with coconut flakes or shredded coconut for a decorative touch.

Blend (Optional):

- For an extra creamy and frothy texture, you can blend the Coconut Iced Coffee using a blender. This step is optional but creates a more indulgent drink.

Serve:

- Serve your Coconut Iced Coffee immediately and enjoy the tropical flavors!

Feel free to experiment with the coffee-to-coconut milk ratio, as well as the level of sweetness, to tailor the Coconut Iced Coffee to your liking. It's a perfect treat for warm days or whenever you crave a hint of the tropics in your coffee.

**Hazelnut Macchiato**

Ingredients:

- Freshly brewed espresso (1-2 shots)
- Hazelnut syrup or hazelnut-flavored coffee syrup (to taste)
- Milk (steamed or frothed)
- Caramel syrup (optional, for drizzling)

Equipment:

- Espresso machine
- Milk frother or steamer
- Spoon for stirring
- Optional: Caramel syrup for garnish

Instructions:

Brew Espresso:

- Brew 1 to 2 shots of espresso using your espresso machine. Ensure the espresso is strong and aromatic.

Prepare Hazelnut Syrup:

- Add hazelnut syrup to the bottom of your serving cup. The amount can vary based on your sweetness preference, but a good starting point is 1-2 tablespoons.

Add Espresso:

- Pour the freshly brewed espresso shots over the hazelnut syrup in the cup.

Steam or Froth Milk:

- Steam or froth the milk using a milk frother or steamer until it reaches a velvety and creamy consistency.

Pour Milk Over Espresso:

- Gently pour the steamed or frothed milk over the espresso and hazelnut syrup mixture. Hold back the foam with a spoon to control the amount of foam in your macchiato.

Optional Caramel Drizzle:

- If you like, drizzle a small amount of caramel syrup over the top of the milk for an extra layer of sweetness and decoration.

Stir (Optional):

- If desired, you can gently stir the hazelnut syrup, espresso, and milk to combine the flavors.

Serve Immediately:

- Hazelnut Macchiato is best enjoyed promptly while the espresso is fresh and the milk is creamy.

Enjoy:

- Sip and savor the delightful combination of hazelnut and espresso in this creamy Hazelnut Macchiato!

Feel free to adjust the hazelnut syrup quantity based on your taste preferences. This recipe offers a balanced blend of nutty sweetness with the boldness of espresso, creating a delicious and indulgent coffee treat.

**Salted Caramel Latte**

Ingredients:

- Freshly brewed espresso (1-2 shots)
- Caramel syrup (2 tablespoons)
- Milk (steamed)
- Pinch of sea salt
- Whipped cream (optional, for topping)
- Caramel sauce (optional, for drizzling)

Equipment:

- Espresso machine
- Milk frother or steamer
- Spoon for stirring
- Optional: Whipped cream dispenser, caramel sauce for garnish

Instructions:

Brew Espresso:
- Brew 1 to 2 shots of espresso using your espresso machine. Ensure the espresso is strong and aromatic.

Heat Milk:
- Steam the milk using a milk frother or steamer until it reaches a creamy and velvety texture.

Add Caramel Syrup:

- In your serving cup, add caramel syrup to the bottom. A good starting point is around 2 tablespoons, but you can adjust it based on your sweetness preference.

Pour Espresso Over Caramel:

- Pour the freshly brewed espresso shots over the caramel syrup in the cup.

Stir to Combine:

- Gently stir the caramel syrup and espresso to ensure they are well combined.

Steam Milk:

- Pour the steamed milk over the espresso and caramel mixture, holding back the foam with a spoon to control the amount of foam in your latte.

Add a Pinch of Sea Salt:

- Sprinkle a pinch of sea salt over the top of the milk. The salt adds a savory element that complements the sweetness of the caramel.

Optional Whipped Cream:

- If you like, top your Salted Caramel Latte with a dollop of whipped cream for an extra indulgent treat.

Optional Caramel Drizzle:

- Drizzle a little extra caramel sauce on top for added sweetness and decoration.

Serve Immediately:

- Salted Caramel Latte is best enjoyed promptly while the espresso is fresh and the milk is creamy.

Enjoy:

- Sip and savor the delightful combination of caramel, salt, and espresso in this delicious Salted Caramel Latte!

Feel free to customize this recipe by adjusting the caramel syrup and salt quantities to suit your taste preferences. It's a perfect choice for those who enjoy a sweet and salty flavor profile in their coffee.

**Pumpkin Spice Latte**

Ingredients:

- 1 cup strong brewed coffee or 1-2 shots of espresso
- 1/2 cup milk (whole milk, almond milk, or your choice)
- 2 tablespoons pumpkin puree
- 1-2 tablespoons sugar (adjust to taste)
- 1/4 teaspoon pumpkin pie spice (cinnamon, nutmeg, ginger, and cloves)
- Whipped cream for topping
- Optional: Vanilla extract for added flavor

Equipment:

- Coffee maker (drip, espresso machine, or French press)
- Saucepan or microwave-safe container
- Whisk or milk frother
- Optional: Handheld blender for frothing

Instructions:

Brew Coffee or Espresso:
- Brew a cup of strong coffee using your preferred method. If using an espresso machine, pull 1-2 shots of espresso.

Heat Milk and Pumpkin Puree:
- In a saucepan or microwave-safe container, heat the milk until it is warm but not boiling. Add the pumpkin puree and whisk until well combined. You can also use a milk frother to froth the milk and pumpkin mixture.

Add Sugar and Spice:

- Stir in sugar, pumpkin pie spice, and optionally, a few drops of vanilla extract. Adjust the sweetness and spice level according to your taste preferences.

Combine Coffee and Pumpkin Milk:

- Pour the brewed coffee or espresso into a mug. Add the warm pumpkin milk mixture to the coffee and stir well.

Optional Froth:

- Use a milk frother or handheld blender to froth the top of the Pumpkin Spice Latte for a creamy texture.

Top with Whipped Cream:

- Dollop whipped cream on top of the latte. You can also sprinkle a bit of pumpkin pie spice or cinnamon for garnish.

Serve Warm:

- Pumpkin Spice Latte is best enjoyed while warm and cozy.

Enjoy:

- Sip and savor the delicious fall flavors of your homemade Pumpkin Spice Latte!

Feel free to customize the recipe by adjusting the sweetness, spice level, or type of milk used. It's a perfect seasonal treat that captures the essence of autumn.

**Maple Pecan Coffee**

Ingredients:

- Freshly ground coffee beans
- Water
- Maple syrup
- Pecans, chopped and toasted
- Milk (optional)
- Whipped cream (optional)
- Ground cinnamon or nutmeg (optional, for garnish)

Equipment:

- Coffee maker (drip, pour-over, or French press)
- Saucepan or microwave-safe container (for toasting pecans)
- Optional: Whipped cream dispenser or hand mixer

Instructions:

Brew Coffee:
- Brew a pot of your favorite coffee using your preferred method. A medium to dark roast works well for this recipe.

Toast Pecans:
- In a saucepan over medium heat or in a microwave-safe container, toast the chopped pecans until they become fragrant and slightly golden. Be careful not to burn them. Set aside.

Prepare Maple Pecan Syrup:

- In a small saucepan, combine maple syrup and the toasted pecans. Heat the mixture over medium-low heat for a few minutes, allowing the pecans to infuse their flavor into the syrup. Stir occasionally.

Sweeten Coffee:

- Add the maple pecan syrup to your brewed coffee, adjusting the amount based on your sweetness preference. Stir well to combine.

Optional Milk:

- If you like, you can add warm milk to your Maple Pecan Coffee for a creamier texture. Heat the milk separately and froth it using a milk frother or a handheld blender if desired.

Optional Whipped Cream:

- Top your Maple Pecan Coffee with a dollop of whipped cream for added richness. You can use a whipped cream dispenser or a hand mixer to whip the cream.

Garnish (Optional):

- Sprinkle a bit of ground cinnamon or nutmeg on top for a festive touch.

Serve Immediately:

- Maple Pecan Coffee is best enjoyed promptly while it's warm and fragrant.

Enjoy:

- Sip and savor the delightful combination of maple, pecans, and coffee in your homemade Maple Pecan Coffee!

Feel free to customize the recipe by adjusting the amount of maple pecan syrup, adding flavored syrups, or experimenting with different types of milk. It's a perfect treat for the fall or any time you crave a cozy and flavorful coffee experience.

**Almond Joy Coffee**

Ingredients:

- Freshly ground coffee beans
- Water
- Sweetened shredded coconut
- Chocolate syrup
- Almond extract
- Milk (optional)
- Whipped cream (optional)
- Sliced almonds (optional, for garnish)

Equipment:

- Coffee maker (drip, pour-over, or espresso machine)
- Optional: Milk frother or steamer
- Optional: Whipped cream dispenser or hand mixer

Instructions:

Brew Coffee:

- Brew a cup of your favorite coffee using your preferred method. A medium to dark roast pairs well with the chocolate and almond flavors.

Prepare Coconut Topping:

- In a small skillet over medium heat, toast the sweetened shredded coconut until it becomes golden brown and fragrant. Stir frequently to prevent burning. Set aside.

Add Chocolate Syrup and Almond Extract:

- While the coffee is brewing, add chocolate syrup to the bottom of your coffee cup. Add a few drops of almond extract to the chocolate syrup, adjusting to your taste preference.

Brew Coffee Over Chocolate Mixture:

- Brew the hot coffee directly over the chocolate syrup and almond extract mixture. This helps to dissolve the chocolate and infuse the coffee with flavor.

Stir Well:

- Stir the coffee, chocolate, and almond extract mixture well to ensure they are thoroughly combined.

Optional Milk Frothing:

- If you enjoy a creamier texture, froth or steam milk using a milk frother or steamer. Add the frothed milk to the coffee.

Top with Toasted Coconut:

- Sprinkle the toasted sweetened shredded coconut over the top of the coffee.

Optional Whipped Cream:

- If desired, top your Almond Joy Coffee with a dollop of whipped cream. You can use a whipped cream dispenser or a hand mixer to whip the cream.

Optional Almond Garnish:

- Garnish with sliced almonds for an extra crunch and visual appeal.

Serve Immediately:

- Almond Joy Coffee is best enjoyed while it's hot and flavorful.

Enjoy:

- Sip and savor the delicious combination of chocolate, coconut, and almonds in your homemade Almond Joy Coffee!

Feel free to customize this recipe by adjusting the chocolate, almond extract, and coconut quantities to suit your taste preferences. It's a delightful way to enjoy the flavors reminiscent of the popular candy bar in a comforting coffee form.

**Gingerbread Latte**

Ingredients:

- Freshly brewed espresso (1-2 shots)
- 1 to 2 tablespoons gingerbread syrup (store-bought or homemade, see recipe below)
- Milk (steamed)
- Whipped cream (optional, for topping)
- Ground cinnamon or nutmeg (optional, for garnish)

Gingerbread Syrup Ingredients:

- 1 cup water
- 1 cup brown sugar
- 1 tablespoon molasses
- 1 tablespoon ground ginger
- 1 teaspoon ground cinnamon
- 1/2 teaspoon ground cloves
- 1/2 teaspoon vanilla extract

Equipment:

- Espresso machine
- Milk frother or steamer
- Saucepan (for syrup)
- Whisk or spoon for stirring
- Optional: Whipped cream dispenser or hand mixer

Instructions:

Gingerbread Syrup:

Combine Ingredients:
- In a saucepan, combine water, brown sugar, molasses, ground ginger, ground cinnamon, and ground cloves.

Simmer:
- Heat the mixture over medium heat, stirring occasionally, until it comes to a simmer. Simmer for a few minutes until the sugar is fully dissolved and the mixture has thickened slightly.

Add Vanilla:
- Remove the saucepan from heat and stir in the vanilla extract. Let the syrup cool before using.

Gingerbread Latte:

Brew Espresso:
- Brew 1 to 2 shots of espresso using your espresso machine.

Add Gingerbread Syrup:
- In your serving cup, add 1 to 2 tablespoons of the prepared gingerbread syrup. Adjust the amount based on your sweetness preference.

Pour Espresso Over Syrup:
- Pour the freshly brewed espresso shots over the gingerbread syrup in the cup.

Steam Milk:

- Steam the milk using a milk frother or steamer until it reaches a creamy and velvety texture.

Add Steamed Milk:

- Pour the steamed milk over the espresso and gingerbread syrup mixture, holding back the foam with a spoon to control the amount of foam in your latte.

Optional Whipped Cream:

- Top your Gingerbread Latte with a dollop of whipped cream for added richness. You can use a whipped cream dispenser or a hand mixer to whip the cream.

Garnish (Optional):

- Sprinkle a bit of ground cinnamon or nutmeg on top for a festive touch.

Serve Immediately:

- Gingerbread Latte is best enjoyed while it's warm and fragrant.

Enjoy:

- Sip and savor the festive and spiced flavors of your homemade Gingerbread Latte!

Feel free to adjust the gingerbread syrup quantity and sweetness level according to your taste preferences. It's a perfect holiday-inspired treat for coffee lovers.

# Tea Recipes:

**Classic Earl Grey Lavender Tea**

Ingredients:

- 1 Earl Grey tea bag or 1 teaspoon loose Earl Grey tea leaves
- 1 teaspoon dried culinary lavender buds (food-grade)
- Hot water
- Optional: Honey or sweetener of your choice
- Optional: Milk or cream

Equipment:

- Teapot or teacup with an infuser
- Tea kettle or hot water dispenser
- Optional: Tea strainer

Instructions:

Boil Water:

- Bring fresh water to a boil. The ideal water temperature for black tea like Earl Grey is around 200-212°F (93-100°C).

Preheat Teapot or Teacup:

- Pour a small amount of hot water into your teapot or teacup to warm it. Swirl the water around and discard it.

Add Tea Leaves and Lavender:

- Place the Earl Grey tea bag or tea leaves and dried lavender buds into the infuser of your teapot or directly into your teacup.

Pour Hot Water:

- Pour the hot water over the tea leaves and lavender. Use the recommended amount of water for your tea bag or tea leaves (usually 1 cup).

Steep the Tea:

- Let the tea steep for about 3 to 5 minutes. Adjust the steeping time based on your preference for tea strength. Earl Grey tea tends to be stronger, so a shorter steeping time is often sufficient.

Optional Sweetening:

- If desired, add honey or your preferred sweetener to the tea, stirring until it dissolves.

Optional Milk or Cream:

- Add milk or cream if you like a creamier tea. Earl Grey Lavender Tea can be enjoyed both with or without milk.

Strain (Optional):

- If you used loose tea leaves, you may need to strain the tea into another cup or teapot to remove the leaves. If you used a tea bag, simply remove the bag.

Serve:

- Pour the infused Earl Grey Lavender Tea into your teacup and serve it hot.

Enjoy:

- Sip and enjoy the aromatic blend of Earl Grey tea with the floral notes of lavender.

The combination of Earl Grey and lavender creates a soothing and elegant tea that is perfect for a calming afternoon or evening ritual. Adjust the lavender quantity based on your personal preference for the floral aroma.

**Chai Latte with Spiced Honey**

Ingredients:

For Spiced Honey:

- 1/2 cup honey
- 1 cinnamon stick
- 3-4 whole cloves
- 1-2 cardamom pods, crushed
- 1 small piece of fresh ginger, sliced

For Chai Latte:

- 2 chai tea bags or 2 tablespoons loose chai tea leaves
- 1 cup water
- 1 cup milk (whole milk, almond milk, or your choice)
- 2 tablespoons spiced honey (prepared as below)
- Optional: Ground cinnamon or nutmeg for garnish

Instructions:

Spiced Honey:

    Prepare Spiced Honey:

- In a small saucepan, combine honey, a cinnamon stick, whole cloves, crushed cardamom pods, and sliced ginger.

    Heat and Infuse:

- Heat the mixture over low heat, stirring occasionally, until the honey becomes warm and infused with the spices. Let it simmer for a few minutes, allowing the flavors to meld.

Strain:
- Once the honey is infused, strain it to remove the spices. Set aside the spiced honey for your Chai Latte.

Chai Latte:

Brew Chai Tea:
- In a saucepan, bring water to a boil. Add the chai tea bags or loose chai tea leaves to the boiling water. Remove from heat and let the tea steep for about 5 minutes.

Heat Milk:
- While the chai tea is steeping, heat the milk in a separate saucepan until it's warm but not boiling. You can also use a milk frother or steamer for a creamier texture.

Combine Chai Tea and Milk:
- Once the chai tea has steeped, remove the tea bags or strain out the loose leaves. Combine the brewed chai tea and warm milk in a saucepan.

Add Spiced Honey:
- Stir in the spiced honey, adjusting the amount based on your sweetness preference.

Optional Frothing:
- If you have a milk frother, you can froth the chai latte for a creamier texture.

Serve:

- Pour the Chai Latte with Spiced Honey into your favorite mug.

Garnish (Optional):

- Sprinkle a bit of ground cinnamon or nutmeg on top for a festive touch.

Enjoy:

- Sip and savor the warm and comforting flavors of your homemade Chai Latte with Spiced Honey!

Feel free to customize the spiced honey quantity and sweetness level according to your taste preferences. This recipe provides a cozy and flavorful twist on the classic Chai Latte.

**Matcha Green Tea Smoothie**

Ingredients:

- 1 teaspoon matcha powder
- 1 banana, frozen
- 1/2 cup plain Greek yogurt
- 1/2 cup almond milk (or any milk of your choice)
- 1 tablespoon honey or maple syrup (optional, for sweetness)
- Ice cubes (optional)
- Fresh mint leaves for garnish (optional)

Equipment:

- Blender

Instructions:

Prepare Matcha:

- In a small bowl, sift the matcha powder to remove any lumps. Add a small amount of hot water (not boiling) to the matcha powder and whisk until it forms a smooth paste. This helps to dissolve the matcha and enhance its flavor.

Combine Ingredients:

- In a blender, combine the matcha paste, frozen banana, Greek yogurt, almond milk, and honey or maple syrup if using. If you prefer a colder and thicker smoothie, you can add a handful of ice cubes.

Blend:

- Blend the ingredients until smooth and creamy. If the smoothie is too thick, you can add more almond milk to reach your desired consistency.

Taste and Adjust:

- Taste the smoothie and adjust the sweetness by adding more honey or maple syrup if needed.

Serve:

- Pour the Matcha Green Tea Smoothie into a glass.

Garnish (Optional):

- Garnish with fresh mint leaves for a burst of freshness and a touch of color.

Enjoy:

- Sip and enjoy the invigorating and nutrient-packed Matcha Green Tea Smoothie!

This smoothie is not only delicious but also provides the health benefits of matcha, which is rich in antioxidants and offers a gentle energy boost. Feel free to customize the recipe by adding other ingredients like spinach, chia seeds, or a splash of citrus juice for additional flavor and nutrition.

**Jasmine Rose White Tea**

Ingredients:

- 1-2 teaspoons white tea leaves (Silver Needle or Bai Hao Yin Zhen are excellent choices)
- 1 teaspoon dried jasmine flowers
- 1 teaspoon dried rose petals
- Hot water (about 175°F or 80°C)
- Honey or sweetener of your choice (optional)

Equipment:

- Teapot or infuser
- Tea kettle
- Teacup

Instructions:

Heat Water:

- Bring water to a temperature of about 175°F (80°C). White tea is delicate, so using water that is too hot can result in a bitter taste.

Rinse Teapot or Infuser:

- Pour a small amount of hot water into your teapot or infuser to warm it. Discard this water.

Add Tea Leaves and Flowers:

- Place the white tea leaves, dried jasmine flowers, and dried rose petals into the teapot or infuser.

Pour Hot Water:

- Pour the hot water over the tea leaves and flowers. Ensure that the water is not boiling; the lower temperature preserves the delicate nature of white tea.

Steep:

- Let the tea steep for about 3-5 minutes. You can adjust the steeping time based on your preference for tea strength. Keep in mind that white tea is subtle, and over-steeping may result in bitterness.

Strain or Remove Infuser:

- Once the tea has steeped, either remove the infuser or strain the tea to separate the leaves and flowers from the liquid.

Sweeten (Optional):

- If you like, add honey or a sweetener of your choice to enhance the flavor. Adjust the sweetness to your preference.

Serve:

- Pour the Jasmine Rose White Tea into your teacup.

Enjoy:

- Sip and enjoy the delicate and floral notes of your homemade Jasmine Rose White Tea!

Feel free to experiment with the tea-to-flower ratio and adjust the sweetness level to suit your taste. This recipe offers a delightful blend of floral aromas and the subtle elegance of white tea.

**Minty Moroccan Mint Tea**

Ingredients:

- 2-3 teaspoons loose green tea leaves (Gunpowder green tea is a common choice)
- 1 bunch fresh mint leaves (about 10-15 sprigs)
- 3-4 tablespoons sugar (adjust to taste)
- Water (about 3 cups)
- Optional: Fresh lemon wedges for serving

Equipment:

- Moroccan tea pot (known as a "teapot" or "tetera")
- Tea glasses or small cups

Instructions:

Prepare Mint:
- Wash the fresh mint leaves thoroughly.

Boil Water:
- In a tea kettle or pot, bring about 3 cups of water to a boil.

Rinse Tea Pot:
- Pour a small amount of hot water into the Moroccan tea pot to warm it. Swirl the water around and discard it.

Add Tea Leaves and Mint:
- Place the green tea leaves and fresh mint leaves in the tea pot.

Add Boiling Water:

- Pour the boiling water into the tea pot over the tea leaves and mint.

Steep:
- Allow the tea leaves and mint to steep for about 3-5 minutes. The longer the steeping time, the stronger the tea.

First Pour:
- To enhance the flavor, pour a small amount of the steeped tea into a glass or cup, then pour it back into the tea pot. Repeat this process two or three times.

Add Sugar:
- Add sugar to the tea pot. The amount of sugar can be adjusted to your taste preferences. In Moroccan tradition, the tea is often sweetened generously.

Second Boiling:
- Return the tea pot to the heat and bring the tea to a second boil. This helps dissolve the sugar and infuse the flavors.

Pour and Serve:
- Pour the Moroccan Mint Tea into tea glasses or small cups from a height to create a frothy layer on top.

Optional Lemon Wedges:
- Serve with fresh lemon wedges on the side. Some people like to add a squeeze of lemon to their tea for extra flavor.

Enjoy:
- Sip and savor the refreshing and minty goodness of Moroccan Mint Tea!

Moroccan Mint Tea is often enjoyed in a ceremonial manner, and it is a symbol of hospitality in Moroccan culture. The process of pouring the tea from a height is not only for show but also to aerate the tea and enhance its flavor. Adjust the sweetness and mintiness according to your preferences.

**Turmeric Ginger Herbal Tea**

Ingredients:

- 1 teaspoon turmeric powder or 1 small turmeric root, peeled and sliced
- 1 teaspoon fresh ginger, grated or sliced
- 1 tablespoon honey (adjust to taste)
- Juice of half a lemon (optional)
- 2 cups water

Optional Add-ins:

- A pinch of black pepper (enhances turmeric absorption)
- Fresh mint leaves
- Cinnamon stick
- 1-2 teaspoons loose herbal tea (such as chamomile or rooibos) for added flavor

Instructions:

Prepare Turmeric and Ginger:
- If using fresh turmeric root, peel and slice it thinly. Grate or slice the fresh ginger.

Boil Water:
- In a saucepan, bring 2 cups of water to a boil.

Add Turmeric and Ginger:
- Add the turmeric and ginger to the boiling water.

Optional Add-ins:

- If using black pepper, mint leaves, cinnamon stick, or loose herbal tea, add them to the water as well.

Simmer:
- Reduce the heat and let the mixture simmer for about 10-15 minutes. This helps extract the flavors and medicinal properties of turmeric and ginger.

Strain:
- After simmering, strain the tea to remove the turmeric and ginger pieces. You can use a fine mesh strainer or cheesecloth.

Sweeten:
- Stir in honey to sweeten the tea. Adjust the sweetness according to your taste preferences.

Optional Lemon Juice:
- Add a squeeze of fresh lemon juice if desired. Lemon adds a citrusy brightness to the tea.

Serve:
- Pour the Turmeric Ginger Herbal Tea into your favorite mug.

Enjoy:
- Sip and enjoy the warm and soothing Turmeric Ginger Herbal Tea!

This herbal tea is not only delicious but also known for its potential health benefits, including anti-inflammatory properties from turmeric and digestive benefits from ginger. Feel free to customize the recipe based on your taste preferences and health goals.

**Berry Hibiscus Iced Tea**

Ingredients:

- 2 hibiscus tea bags
- 1 cup mixed berries (strawberries, blueberries, raspberries)
- 2 tablespoons honey or sweetener of your choice
- Ice cubes
- Fresh mint leaves for garnish (optional)
- Lemon slices for garnish (optional)

Instructions:

Brew Hibiscus Tea:

- Place the hibiscus tea bags in a heatproof container. Bring 2 cups of water to a boil and pour it over the tea bags. Let it steep for about 5-7 minutes.

Sweeten Tea:

- Stir in honey or your preferred sweetener while the tea is still warm. Adjust the sweetness to your liking.

Cool Tea:

- Allow the hibiscus tea to cool to room temperature, then refrigerate it until it's chilled.

Prepare Berries:

- Wash and slice the mixed berries. You can choose a combination of strawberries, blueberries, and raspberries.

Assemble Iced Tea:

- Fill a glass with ice cubes. Add a generous amount of the sliced mixed berries to the glass.

Pour Chilled Hibiscus Tea:

- Pour the chilled hibiscus tea over the ice and berries.

Stir:

- Gently stir the iced tea to mix the flavors and distribute the berries.

Garnish (Optional):

- Garnish the Berry Hibiscus Iced Tea with fresh mint leaves or lemon slices for added freshness.

Serve:

- Serve the Berry Hibiscus Iced Tea immediately.

Enjoy:

- Sip and enjoy the fruity and floral goodness of your homemade Berry Hibiscus Iced Tea!

Feel free to experiment with the berry combination and sweetness level based on your taste preferences. This iced tea is not only delicious but also visually appealing with the vibrant colors of the berries. It's perfect for warm days or as a refreshing pick-me-up.

**Berry Hibiscus Iced Tea**

Ingredients:

- 4 hibiscus tea bags
- 1 cup mixed berries (strawberries, blueberries, raspberries)
- 2 tablespoons honey or sweetener of your choice
- Ice cubes
- Fresh mint leaves for garnish (optional)
- Lemon slices for garnish (optional)

Instructions:

Brew Hibiscus Tea:
- Place the hibiscus tea bags in a heatproof container. Bring 4 cups of water to a boil and pour it over the tea bags. Let it steep for about 5-7 minutes.

Sweeten Tea:
- Stir in honey or your preferred sweetener while the tea is still warm. Adjust the sweetness to your liking.

Cool Tea:
- Allow the hibiscus tea to cool to room temperature, then refrigerate it until it's chilled.

Prepare Berries:
- Wash and slice the mixed berries. You can choose a combination of strawberries, blueberries, and raspberries.

Assemble Iced Tea:

- Fill glasses with ice cubes. Add a generous amount of the sliced mixed berries to each glass.

Pour Chilled Hibiscus Tea:

- Pour the chilled hibiscus tea over the ice and berries.

Stir:

- Gently stir the iced tea in each glass to mix the flavors and distribute the berries.

Garnish (Optional):

- Garnish the Berry Hibiscus Iced Tea with fresh mint leaves or lemon slices for added freshness.

Serve:

- Serve the Berry Hibiscus Iced Tea immediately.

Enjoy:

- Sip and enjoy the fruity and floral goodness of your homemade Berry Hibiscus Iced Tea!

Feel free to customize the recipe by adjusting the amount of berries, sweetness level, or adding other fruits if you like. This refreshing iced tea is perfect for hot days or as a delightful and colorful beverage for any occasion.

**Lemon Chamomile Relaxation Tea**

Ingredients:

- 1 chamomile tea bag or 1 tablespoon dried chamomile flowers
- 1 slice of fresh lemon
- 1 teaspoon honey or sweetener of your choice (optional)
- Hot water (about 8 ounces)

Equipment:

- Teacup
- Kettle or hot water dispenser

Instructions:

Boil Water:

- Bring about 8 ounces of water to a boil using a kettle or hot water dispenser.

Prepare Chamomile Tea:

- Place the chamomile tea bag or dried chamomile flowers in your teacup.

Add Lemon Slice:

- Add a slice of fresh lemon to the teacup. Squeeze it slightly to release some juice.

Pour Hot Water:

- Pour the boiling water over the chamomile tea bag or flowers and lemon slice in the teacup.

Steep:

- Let the tea steep for about 5 minutes. This allows the chamomile to infuse into the water, creating a relaxing and aromatic tea.

Sweeten (Optional):

- If desired, add honey or your preferred sweetener to the tea. Stir until it dissolves.

Remove Tea Bag or Strain (If Using Flowers):

- If using a tea bag, remove it from the teacup. If using dried chamomile flowers, strain the tea to remove the flowers.

Optional Lemon Garnish:

- Garnish with an additional lemon slice if you wish.

Stir and Enjoy:

- Give the tea a gentle stir and enjoy the calming Lemon Chamomile Relaxation Tea.

This tea is known for its soothing properties, making it a perfect choice for relaxation and promoting better sleep. The combination of chamomile and lemon adds a pleasant flavor to the tea. Adjust the sweetness and lemon quantity based on your taste preferences. It's a wonderful way to unwind and create a peaceful moment before bedtime.

**Peach Basil White Tea Cooler**

Ingredients:

- 2 teaspoons white tea leaves (Silver Needle or Bai Hao Yin Zhen work well)
- 1 ripe peach, sliced
- Handful of fresh basil leaves
- 1-2 tablespoons honey or sweetener of your choice
- Ice cubes
- Water (about 2 cups)
- Optional: Peach slices and basil leaves for garnish

Equipment:

- Teapot or infuser
- Blender

Instructions:

Prepare White Tea:
- Place the white tea leaves in a teapot or infuser. Bring 2 cups of water to a temperature of about 175°F (80°C). Pour the hot water over the tea leaves and let it steep for 3-5 minutes. Strain the tea and let it cool to room temperature.

Blend Peach and Basil:
- In a blender, combine the sliced peach, fresh basil leaves, and honey. Blend until you get a smooth puree.

Combine Tea and Peach Basil Puree:

- In a large pitcher, combine the cooled white tea with the peach basil puree. Stir well to mix the flavors.

Strain (Optional):

- If you prefer a smoother texture, you can strain the mixture using a fine mesh strainer to remove any pulp. This step is optional.

Chill:

- Place the pitcher in the refrigerator to chill the Peach Basil White Tea Cooler for at least 1-2 hours.

Serve Over Ice:

- Fill glasses with ice cubes and pour the chilled Peach Basil White Tea Cooler over the ice.

Garnish (Optional):

- Garnish each glass with additional peach slices and basil leaves for a visually appealing touch.

Stir Before Serving:

- Give the cooler a gentle stir before serving to ensure that the flavors are well-mixed.

Enjoy:

- Sip and enjoy the Peach Basil White Tea Cooler for a refreshing and flavorful experience!

Feel free to adjust the sweetness by adding more or less honey, depending on your taste preferences. This cooler is a wonderful way to enjoy the combination of white tea, sweet peaches, and aromatic basil, especially on a warm day.

**Lavender Blueberry Green Tea**

Ingredients:

- 2 teaspoons green tea leaves (Sencha or Dragonwell work well)
- 1 teaspoon dried lavender buds (culinary-grade)
- 1/2 cup fresh blueberries
- Honey or sweetener of your choice (optional)
- Water (about 2 cups)
- Ice cubes (optional)

Equipment:

- Teapot or infuser
- Fine mesh strainer
- Blender (optional)

Instructions:

Prepare Green Tea:
- Place the green tea leaves in a teapot or infuser. Bring 2 cups of water to a temperature of about 175°F (80°C). Pour the hot water over the green tea leaves and let it steep for 2-3 minutes. Strain the tea and let it cool to room temperature.

Blend Blueberries and Lavender:
- In a blender, combine the fresh blueberries and dried lavender buds. Blend until you get a smooth puree.

Combine Tea and Blueberry Lavender Puree:
- In a pitcher, combine the cooled green tea with the blueberry lavender puree. Stir well to mix the flavors.

Strain (Optional):

- If you prefer a smoother texture, you can strain the mixture using a fine mesh strainer to remove any pulp. This step is optional.

Sweeten (Optional):

- Add honey or your preferred sweetener to the tea, adjusting the sweetness to your liking. Stir until the sweetener is dissolved.

Chill:

- Place the pitcher in the refrigerator to chill the Lavender Blueberry Green Tea for at least 1-2 hours.

Serve Over Ice (Optional):

- If desired, you can serve the tea over ice cubes for a refreshing iced tea experience.

Garnish (Optional):

- Garnish with a few whole blueberries or a sprig of fresh lavender for a decorative touch.

Stir Before Serving:

- Give the tea a gentle stir before serving to ensure that the flavors are well-mixed.

Enjoy:

- Sip and enjoy the fragrant and flavorful Lavender Blueberry Green Tea!

Feel free to experiment with the lavender and blueberry quantities to suit your taste preferences. This tea is a lovely way to combine the antioxidant-rich properties of green tea with the natural sweetness of blueberries and the calming aroma of lavender.

**Lavender Blueberry Green Tea**

Ingredients:

- 2 teaspoons green tea leaves (Sencha or Dragonwell are good choices)
- 1 teaspoon dried culinary lavender buds
- 1/2 cup fresh blueberries
- Honey or sweetener of your choice (optional)
- Water (about 2 cups)
- Ice cubes (optional)

Equipment:

- Teapot or infuser
- Fine mesh strainer
- Blender (optional)

Instructions:

Prepare Green Tea:
- Place the green tea leaves in a teapot or infuser. Bring 2 cups of water to a temperature of about 175°F (80°C). Pour the hot water over the green tea leaves and let it steep for 2-3 minutes. Strain the tea and allow it to cool to room temperature.

Blend Blueberries and Lavender:
- In a blender, combine the fresh blueberries and dried lavender buds. Blend until you get a smooth puree.

Combine Tea and Blueberry Lavender Puree:
- In a pitcher, combine the cooled green tea with the blueberry lavender puree. Stir well to mix the flavors.

Strain (Optional):

- If you prefer a smoother texture, you can strain the mixture using a fine mesh strainer to remove any pulp. This step is optional.

Sweeten (Optional):
- Add honey or your preferred sweetener to the tea, adjusting the sweetness to your liking. Stir until the sweetener is dissolved.

Chill:
- Place the pitcher in the refrigerator to chill the Lavender Blueberry Green Tea for at least 1-2 hours.

Serve Over Ice (Optional):
- If desired, you can serve the tea over ice cubes for a refreshing iced tea experience.

Garnish (Optional):
- Garnish with a few whole blueberries or a sprig of fresh lavender for a decorative touch.

Stir Before Serving:
- Give the tea a gentle stir before serving to ensure that the flavors are well-mixed.

Enjoy:
- Sip and enjoy the fragrant and flavorful Lavender Blueberry Green Tea!

Feel free to customize the lavender and blueberry quantities to suit your taste preferences. This tea is a delightful combination of the antioxidant-rich properties of green tea, the natural sweetness of blueberries, and the aromatic essence of lavender.

**Masala Rooibos Chai**

Ingredients:

- 2 teaspoons loose rooibos tea or 2 rooibos tea bags
- 3-4 green cardamom pods, crushed
- 1 cinnamon stick
- 4-5 cloves
- 1-inch piece of fresh ginger, sliced
- 1-2 black peppercorns (optional, for a bit of heat)
- 1-2 tablespoons honey or sweetener of your choice
- 1 cup milk (dairy or non-dairy)
- Water (2 cups)
- Optional: Star anise, nutmeg, or fennel seeds for additional spice

Instructions:

Prepare Masala Chai Spice Blend:

- In a mortar and pestle, crush the cardamom pods, cinnamon stick, cloves, and black peppercorns (if using). You can also use pre-ground spices if you prefer.

Boil Water and Add Spices:

- In a saucepan, bring 2 cups of water to a boil. Add the crushed spice blend and sliced ginger to the boiling water.

Add Rooibos Tea:

- Add the rooibos tea leaves or tea bags to the boiling water and spices. Reduce the heat to low and let it simmer for about 5-7 minutes.

Add Milk:

- Pour in the milk of your choice (dairy or non-dairy) and continue simmering for an additional 5 minutes. Be careful not to let it boil over.

Strain:

- Strain the Masala Rooibos Chai into cups, removing the tea leaves or bags and the whole spices.

Sweeten:

- Stir in honey or your preferred sweetener to taste. Adjust the sweetness according to your preference.

Optional Spice Variation:

- For an extra layer of flavor, you can add a pinch of ground nutmeg, a star anise, or a few fennel seeds during the simmering process.

Serve:

- Pour the Masala Rooibos Chai into your favorite cups or mugs.

Enjoy:

- Sip and enjoy the warm and comforting flavors of Masala Rooibos Chai!

Feel free to experiment with the spice quantities to suit your taste. Masala Rooibos Chai offers a unique and flavorful twist on traditional chai, and the rooibos tea adds a natural sweetness to the blend.

**Coconut Almond Black Chai**

Ingredients:

- 2 teaspoons black tea leaves (Assam or Darjeeling work well)
- 3-4 green cardamom pods, crushed
- 1 cinnamon stick
- 4-5 cloves
- 1-inch piece of fresh ginger, sliced
- 1-2 black peppercorns (optional, for a bit of heat)
- 1-2 tablespoons coconut flakes
- 1-2 tablespoons almond slices or chopped almonds
- 1-2 tablespoons honey or sweetener of your choice
- 1 cup milk (dairy or non-dairy)
- Water (2 cups)

Instructions:

Prepare Chai Spice Blend:
- In a mortar and pestle, crush the cardamom pods, cinnamon stick, cloves, and black peppercorns (if using). You can also use pre-ground spices if you prefer.

Boil Water and Add Spices:
- In a saucepan, bring 2 cups of water to a boil. Add the crushed spice blend, sliced ginger, coconut flakes, and almond slices to the boiling water.

Add Black Tea:

- Add the black tea leaves to the boiling water and spices. Reduce the heat to low and let it simmer for about 5-7 minutes.

Add Milk:

- Pour in the milk of your choice (dairy or non-dairy) and continue simmering for an additional 5 minutes. Be careful not to let it boil over.

Strain:

- Strain the Coconut Almond Black Chai into cups, removing the tea leaves and spices.

Sweeten:

- Stir in honey or your preferred sweetener to taste. Adjust the sweetness according to your preference.

Optional Garnish:

- Garnish each cup with a sprinkle of coconut flakes and almond slices for extra flavor and presentation.

Serve:

- Pour the Coconut Almond Black Chai into your favorite cups or mugs.

Enjoy:

- Sip and enjoy the rich and nutty flavors of Coconut Almond Black Chai!

Feel free to adjust the spice quantities and the amount of coconut and almond based on your taste preferences. This chai variation provides a cozy and comforting blend of traditional chai spices with the tropical goodness of coconut and the nutty richness of almonds.

**Vanilla Rooibos Latte**

Ingredients:

- 2 teaspoons loose rooibos tea or 2 rooibos tea bags
- 1 cup milk (dairy or non-dairy)
- 1-2 tablespoons vanilla syrup or 1 teaspoon pure vanilla extract
- Honey or sweetener of your choice (optional)
- Optional: Whipped cream or a sprinkle of cinnamon for garnish

Equipment:

- Teapot or infuser
- Saucepan
- Frother or whisk
- Mug

Instructions:

Prepare Rooibos Tea:

- Place the rooibos tea leaves or tea bags in a teapot or infuser. Bring water to a boil and pour it over the rooibos. Let it steep for about 5-7 minutes.

Heat Milk:

- While the tea is steeping, heat the milk in a saucepan over medium heat. Be careful not to boil it; you want it warm but not scalding.

Froth the Milk:

- Froth the warm milk using a frother or whisk to create a creamy texture. If using a frother, heat the milk until it's almost boiling, then froth it.

Combine Tea and Milk:

- Pour the steeped rooibos tea into a mug. Add the vanilla syrup or vanilla extract to the tea.

Add Frothed Milk:

- Pour the frothed milk over the rooibos tea, holding back the foam with a spoon if you prefer more of a layered latte.

Sweeten (Optional):

- If desired, add honey or your preferred sweetener to taste. Stir until the sweetener is dissolved.

Optional Garnish:

- Top your Vanilla Rooibos Latte with whipped cream or a sprinkle of cinnamon for an extra touch of flavor.

Serve:

- Serve the Vanilla Rooibos Latte while it's warm and comforting.

Enjoy:

- Sip and enjoy the delightful combination of rooibos and vanilla flavors in your latte!

Feel free to adjust the vanilla and sweetness levels according to your taste preferences. This Vanilla Rooibos Latte is a soothing and caffeine-free alternative, perfect for a cozy and relaxing beverage.

**Ginger Peach Turmeric Iced Tea**

Ingredients:

- 2-3 peach tea bags (or 2-3 tablespoons of loose peach tea)
- 1-inch piece of fresh ginger, sliced
- 1 teaspoon ground turmeric or 1 tablespoon fresh turmeric, grated
- 2 tablespoons honey or sweetener of your choice (adjust to taste)
- 4 cups hot water
- Ice cubes
- Peach slices and fresh mint for garnish (optional)

Instructions:

Prepare Peach Tea:

- Place the peach tea bags or loose peach tea in a heatproof container. Pour 4 cups of hot water over the tea and let it steep for about 5-7 minutes.

Add Ginger and Turmeric:

- Add the sliced ginger and ground turmeric (or grated fresh turmeric) to the hot peach tea. Stir well to combine.

Sweeten:

- Stir in honey or your preferred sweetener while the tea is still warm. Adjust the sweetness to your liking.

Cool:

- Allow the tea to cool to room temperature, and then refrigerate it until it's chilled.

Strain:

- Strain the tea to remove the tea bags, loose tea, ginger slices, and any turmeric particles. You can use a fine mesh strainer or cheesecloth.

Serve Over Ice:
- Fill glasses with ice cubes and pour the chilled Ginger Peach Turmeric Iced Tea over the ice.

Garnish (Optional):
- Garnish each glass with peach slices and fresh mint for a visually appealing touch.

Stir Before Serving:
- Give the iced tea a gentle stir before serving to ensure that the flavors are well-mixed.

Enjoy:
- Sip and enjoy the refreshing and invigorating Ginger Peach Turmeric Iced Tea!

Feel free to adjust the ginger, turmeric, and sweetness levels according to your taste preferences. This iced tea not only offers a delightful combination of flavors but also incorporates the potential health benefits of ginger and turmeric.

**Citrus Mint Green Tea Punch**

Ingredients:

- 4 green tea bags
- 4 cups hot water
- 1/2 cup fresh mint leaves, loosely packed
- 1 orange, thinly sliced
- 1 lemon, thinly sliced
- 1 lime, thinly sliced
- 1/4 cup honey or sweetener of your choice (adjust to taste)
- Ice cubes
- Sparkling water (optional, for added fizz)
- Fresh mint sprigs for garnish

Instructions:

Prepare Green Tea:
- Place the green tea bags in a heatproof container. Pour 4 cups of hot water over the tea bags and let them steep for about 3-5 minutes. Remove the tea bags and allow the tea to cool to room temperature.

Muddle Mint:
- In a large pitcher, muddle the fresh mint leaves to release their flavor. You can use a muddler or the back of a spoon for this.

Add Citrus Slices:
- Add the thinly sliced orange, lemon, and lime to the pitcher with the muddled mint.

Sweeten:
- Stir in honey or your preferred sweetener into the cooled green tea. Adjust the sweetness to your liking.

Combine Ingredients:
- Pour the sweetened green tea into the pitcher with the muddled mint and citrus slices. Stir well to combine.

Chill:
- Refrigerate the Citrus Mint Green Tea Punch for at least 1-2 hours to allow the flavors to meld.

Serve Over Ice:
- Fill glasses with ice cubes and pour the chilled punch over the ice.

Optional Sparkling Water:
- For a fizzy twist, top each glass with a splash of sparkling water just before serving.

Garnish:
- Garnish each glass with a fresh mint sprig for an extra burst of aroma.

Stir Before Serving:
- Give the punch a gentle stir before serving to ensure that the flavors are well-distributed.

Enjoy:
- Sip and enjoy the vibrant and cooling Citrus Mint Green Tea Punch!

This punch is perfect for serving at gatherings, parties, or as a refreshing beverage on a warm day. Adjust the sweetness and mint levels based on your preferences.

**Cucumber Basil White Tea Refresher**

Ingredients:

- 2 white tea bags
- 4 cups hot water
- 1/2 cucumber, thinly sliced
- Handful of fresh basil leaves
- 1-2 tablespoons honey or sweetener of your choice (adjust to taste)
- Ice cubes
- Lemon slices for garnish (optional)

Instructions:

Prepare White Tea:
- Place the white tea bags in a heatproof container. Pour 4 cups of hot water over the tea bags and let them steep for about 3-5 minutes. Remove the tea bags and allow the tea to cool to room temperature.

Slice Cucumber and Basil:
- Thinly slice the cucumber and tear the basil leaves into smaller pieces.

Muddle Basil:
- In a large pitcher, muddle the fresh basil leaves to release their aroma. You can use a muddler or the back of a spoon for this.

Add Cucumber Slices:
- Add the thinly sliced cucumber to the pitcher with the muddled basil.

Sweeten:

- Stir in honey or your preferred sweetener into the cooled white tea. Adjust the sweetness to your liking.

Combine Ingredients:

- Pour the sweetened white tea into the pitcher with the muddled basil and cucumber. Stir well to combine.

Chill:

- Refrigerate the Cucumber Basil White Tea Refresher for at least 1-2 hours to enhance the flavors.

Serve Over Ice:

- Fill glasses with ice cubes and pour the chilled refresher over the ice.

Garnish (Optional):

- Garnish each glass with a slice of lemon for an extra citrusy touch.

Stir Before Serving:

- Give the refresher a gentle stir before serving to distribute the cucumber and basil evenly.

Enjoy:

- Sip and enjoy the crisp and rejuvenating Cucumber Basil White Tea Refresher!

Feel free to adjust the sweetness and herb quantities according to your taste preferences. This refresher is a wonderful choice for a light and hydrating drink, perfect for warm days or as a refreshing pick-me-up.

**Rose Cardamom Black Tea Elixir**

Ingredients:

- 2 teaspoons black tea leaves (Assam or Darjeeling work well)
- 3-4 green cardamom pods, crushed
- 1 tablespoon dried rose petals (culinary-grade)
- 1-2 tablespoons honey or sweetener of your choice (adjust to taste)
- 2 cups hot water
- 1-2 teaspoons rose water (optional, for enhanced floral aroma)
- Ice cubes (optional)
- Rose petals for garnish (optional)

Instructions:

Prepare Black Tea:

- Place the black tea leaves in a teapot or infuser. Pour 2 cups of hot water over the tea leaves and let it steep for about 3-5 minutes.

Add Cardamom and Rose Petals:

- Add the crushed cardamom pods and dried rose petals to the hot black tea. Stir gently to combine.

Sweeten:

- Stir in honey or your preferred sweetener while the tea is still warm. Adjust the sweetness to your liking.

Optional Rose Water:

- If you desire a more pronounced floral aroma, add 1-2 teaspoons of rose water to the tea. Stir well.

Strain:
- Strain the Rose Cardamom Black Tea Elixir to remove the tea leaves, cardamom pods, and rose petals. You can use a fine mesh strainer or a tea infuser.

Chill (Optional):
- If you prefer a cold elixir, refrigerate the strained tea for at least 1-2 hours.

Serve:
- Pour the Rose Cardamom Black Tea Elixir into cups. Add ice cubes if you want a chilled beverage.

Garnish (Optional):
- Garnish each cup with a few additional rose petals for a decorative touch.

Stir Before Serving:
- Give the elixir a gentle stir before serving to ensure that the flavors are well-mixed.

Enjoy:
- Sip and savor the unique blend of black tea, cardamom, and rose in this delightful elixir!

Feel free to adjust the cardamom, rose, and sweetness levels based on your taste preferences. This elixir offers a captivating combination of floral and spice notes, making it a perfect choice for a special and aromatic tea experience.

**Pineapple Ginger Herbal Infusion**

Ingredients:

- 1 cup fresh pineapple chunks (or canned pineapple chunks)
- 1-inch piece of fresh ginger, sliced
- 1-2 tablespoons honey or sweetener of your choice (adjust to taste)
- 4 cups hot water
- Fresh mint leaves for garnish (optional)
- Ice cubes (optional)

Instructions:

Prepare Pineapple Ginger Infusion:

- In a heatproof container, combine the fresh pineapple chunks and sliced ginger.

Boil Water:

- Bring 4 cups of water to a boil.

Pour Hot Water Over Ingredients:

- Pour the hot water over the pineapple chunks and ginger. Let it steep for about 10-15 minutes to infuse the flavors.

Sweeten:

- Stir in honey or your preferred sweetener into the infusion. Adjust the sweetness to your liking.

Strain:

- Strain the Pineapple Ginger Herbal Infusion to remove the pineapple chunks and ginger. You can use a fine mesh strainer or cheesecloth.

Chill (Optional):

- If you prefer a cold infusion, refrigerate the strained liquid for at least 1-2 hours.

Serve:

- Pour the Pineapple Ginger Herbal Infusion into cups. Add ice cubes if you want a chilled beverage.

Garnish (Optional):

- Garnish each cup with fresh mint leaves for a burst of freshness.

Stir Before Serving:

- Give the infusion a gentle stir before serving to ensure that the flavors are well-mixed.

Enjoy:

- Sip and enjoy the tropical and soothing Pineapple Ginger Herbal Infusion!

Feel free to adjust the ginger and sweetness levels according to your taste preferences. This infusion is not only delicious but also provides the potential health benefits of ginger and the natural sweetness of pineapple.

**Maple Pecan Oolong Tea**

Ingredients:

- 2 teaspoons oolong tea leaves (or 2 oolong tea bags)
- 1/4 cup pecans, chopped
- 1-2 tablespoons maple syrup (adjust to taste)
- 2 cups hot water
- 1/2 cup milk (dairy or non-dairy)
- Optional: Whipped cream or a sprinkle of cinnamon for garnish

Instructions:

Prepare Oolong Tea:
- Place the oolong tea leaves in a teapot or infuser. Pour 2 cups of hot water over the tea leaves and let it steep for about 3-5 minutes. Remove the tea leaves or bags and set aside.

Toast Pecans:
- In a small pan over medium heat, toast the chopped pecans until they become fragrant and slightly golden. Stir frequently to prevent burning.

Add Pecans to Tea:
- Add the toasted pecans to the brewed oolong tea. This will allow the flavors to infuse.

Sweeten with Maple Syrup:
- Stir in the maple syrup into the tea and pecan mixture. Adjust the sweetness according to your liking.

Heat Milk:

- In a separate saucepan, heat the milk until it's warm but not boiling.

**Froth Milk (Optional):**
- If desired, froth the warm milk using a frother or whisk to create a creamy texture.

**Combine Tea and Milk:**
- Pour the maple pecan-infused oolong tea into cups. Add the frothed milk on top of the tea.

**Optional Garnish:**
- Garnish each cup with a dollop of whipped cream or a sprinkle of cinnamon for an extra touch of indulgence.

**Stir Before Serving:**
- Give the Maple Pecan Oolong Tea a gentle stir before serving to ensure that the flavors are well-mixed.

**Enjoy:**
- Sip and savor the delightful combination of maple, pecans, and oolong in this cozy tea!

Feel free to adjust the pecan and maple syrup quantities based on your taste preferences. This flavored oolong tea is a comforting and indulgent treat, perfect for a cozy afternoon or as a dessert tea.

**Blue Butterfly Pea Flower Tea**

Ingredients:

- 1-2 teaspoons dried butterfly pea flowers (available at tea shops or online)
- 1 cup hot water
- Honey or sweetener of your choice (optional)
- Lemon or lime wedge (optional, for color-changing effect)

Instructions:

Prepare Butterfly Pea Flowers:

- Place the dried butterfly pea flowers in a teapot or infuser.

Pour Hot Water:

- Heat 1 cup of water to near boiling. Pour the hot water over the butterfly pea flowers.

Steep:

- Allow the flowers to steep in the hot water for about 5-10 minutes. The longer you steep, the richer the blue color will be.

Strain:

- Strain the tea to remove the butterfly pea flowers. You can use a fine mesh strainer or remove the infuser.

Sweeten (Optional):

- If desired, add honey or your preferred sweetener to the tea. Stir until the sweetener is dissolved.

Add Citrus (Optional):

- Squeeze a wedge of lemon or lime into the tea. The acidity will cause the blue tea to turn into a beautiful purple or pink color. It's a fun and magical effect!

Serve:

- Pour the Blue Butterfly Pea Flower Tea into a cup.

Enjoy:

- Sip and enjoy the unique flavor and mesmerizing color of Blue Butterfly Pea Flower Tea!

Note: Butterfly pea flower tea is known for its ability to change color in the presence of acidity. Adding lemon or lime will turn the blue tea into shades of purple or pink, creating a visually appealing and dynamic experience.

Feel free to experiment with the steeping time and the amount of butterfly pea flowers to adjust the intensity of both color and flavor. This tea is not only beautiful but also contains antioxidants and is believed to have various health benefits.

**Chocolate Mint Rooibos Bliss**

Ingredients:

- 2 teaspoons rooibos tea leaves or 2 rooibos tea bags
- 1-2 teaspoons cocoa powder (unsweetened)
- 1/4 teaspoon peppermint extract or a handful of fresh mint leaves
- 1-2 tablespoons honey or sweetener of your choice (adjust to taste)
- 2 cups hot water
- 1/2 cup milk (dairy or non-dairy)
- Optional: Whipped cream or chocolate shavings for garnish

Instructions:

Prepare Rooibos Tea:
- Place the rooibos tea leaves or tea bags in a teapot or infuser. Pour 2 cups of hot water over the rooibos and let it steep for about 5-7 minutes.

Add Cocoa Powder:
- Stir in the unsweetened cocoa powder into the hot rooibos tea. Mix well to ensure the cocoa powder is fully dissolved.

Add Peppermint:
- Add the peppermint extract or fresh mint leaves to the tea. If using fresh mint, muddle the leaves slightly to release their flavor.

Sweeten:
- Stir in honey or your preferred sweetener into the tea. Adjust the sweetness to your liking.

Heat Milk:

- In a separate saucepan, heat the milk until it's warm but not boiling.

Froth Milk (Optional):

- If desired, froth the warm milk using a frother or whisk to create a creamy texture.

Combine Tea and Milk:

- Pour the chocolate mint-infused rooibos tea into cups. Add the frothed milk on top of the tea.

Optional Garnish:

- Garnish each cup with a dollop of whipped cream or a sprinkle of chocolate shavings for an extra touch of indulgence.

Stir Before Serving:

- Give the Chocolate Mint Rooibos Bliss a gentle stir before serving to ensure that the flavors are well-mixed.

Enjoy:

- Sip and indulge in the delightful combination of chocolate, mint, and rooibos in this blissful tea!

Feel free to adjust the cocoa powder, mint, and sweetness levels based on your taste preferences. This tea is a cozy and flavorful treat, perfect for a soothing moment of relaxation.